# Boredom BUSTERS for Birds
## 40 Fun and Feather-Friendly Toys and Adventures
By Nikki Moustaki

BOWTIE
PRESS®
A Division of BowTie, Inc.
Irvine, CA

*Vice President, Chief Content Officer:* June Kikuchi
*Vice President, Kennel Club Books:* Andrew DePrisco
*Production Supervisor:* Jessica Jaensch
*Production Coordinator:* Tracy Vogtman
*Art Director:* Cindy Kassebaum
*BowTie Press:* Jennifer Calvert, Amy Deputato,
Lindsay Hanks, Karen Julian, Roger Sipe, Jarelle S. Stein

The author would like to thank *BirdTalk*® Editor Laura Doering.

Library of Congress Cataloging-in-Publication Data
Moustaki, Nikki, 1970–
  Boredom busters for birds : 40 fun and feather-friendly toys and activities / by Nikki Moustaki.
    p. cm.
  Includes bibliographical references.
  ISBN 978-1-935484-19-6
 1.  Birds--Behavior. 2.  Birds--Training.  I. Title.
  SF461.6.M678 2010
  636.6'8--dc22
                        2010000138

BowTie Press®
A Division of BowTie, Inc.
3 Burroughs
Irvine, California 92618

Printed and bound in China
14 13 12 11     3 4 5 6 7 8 9 10

# Table of
# CONTENTS

# Enriching Your BIRD'S LIFE

O ne week your bird is as happy as a hound at an all-you-can-eat buffet, and the next he's biting, screaming, or pulling out his feathers. What happened? The change was so sudden, so unexpected, so unlike him. Has he lost his feathered mind? Maybe he's just bored.

Birds who are physically and mentally unchallenged begin to exhibit unpleasant characteristics and behaviors. They can become depressed, anxious, self-destructive, outwardly aggressive, unpredictable, loud (or conversely, brooding and quiet), and even ill. A bored, lonely

bird may change from a lively and contented pal into something resembling an unruly teenager you wouldn't trust with your car keys. It's time for an enrichment intervention to turn Birdzilla back into a happy, friendly companion.

Lack of enrichment can cause boredom, stress, and anxiety, leading to behavioral problems such as constant screeching, aggression, or feather destruction (plucking, picking, or chewing). Adding enriching toys and activities to a bird's life can solve many such issues and can help prevent a bird from becoming overweight or antisocial.

Enrichment for birds is anything that keeps birds active and engaged in their environment and that stimulates their natural behaviors and instincts. This book explores some simple ways to provide your bird with stimulating types of enrichment to keep him happy, healthy, and out of trouble.

# Enrichment Types
## AND DEFINING FACTORS

There are many ways that you can enrich your bird's life and make his daily routine more varied and interesting. Those ways fall into four categories, or types, of enrichment: solo, social, environmental, and variance. Which enrichment endeavors your bird will respond to depends on a variety of factors, including his species, his age, and his upbringing and general lifestyle. Finding the toys and activities that will capture your bird's attention will also be a matter of trial and error, as no two birds are alike, even those of the same species; what one conure may respond to, for example, another may not.

## The Four Types

Bird enrichment will be most effective if you choose activities from each of the four categories: solo, social, environmental, and variance. Each type of enrichment offers your bird something unique.

**Solo**: Solo activities encourage your bird to engage in an activity by himself. It's critical for a bird to learn to play alone happily and safely. Solo activities should target your bird's particular motivations; you need to discover what activities he finds the most rewarding and fun. Some birds are motivated by chewing and will like toys such as wooden blocks and knotted rope; some birds are motivated by food and will respond to toys and games involving tasty treats; and others are motivated by natural bird behaviors and will appreciate additions to their enclosures that offer such activities as foraging or climbing. Most birds have a variety of motivations that you can tap into to create solo enrichment activities.

**Social**: Social enrichment involves interaction with human family members and possibly with other birds. Social activities include training, hands-on play, and simply hanging out together.

## ☑ Hands-on Play

Some passerine birds, such as finches and canaries, are unlikely to want any hands-on attention from humans. Try simply hanging out together and enjoying some hands-off social interaction instead.

A yellow-collared macaw enjoys some solo time with his colorful toys. Solo activities help birds learn to play alone safely.

# Routine Enrichment

Birds like routine. Knowing what to expect is a big deal for a bird. In the wild, the sun comes up and goes down predictably; there are predictable activities to do and predictable circumstances to handle. In a home, your bird's life should also have routine, but that doesn't mean it has to be stagnant. Find the enriching activities your bird enjoys—whether it be playing solo with his favorite toys, interacting with a friendly birdy playmate, or simply spending time with his favorite human—and make sure they are a regular part of his life.

**Environmental**: Enriching your bird's environment stimulates natural behaviors during the day that help alleviate boredom. Environmental enrichment may include improving your bird's housing and adding a number of interesting elements to the surrounding area.

**Variance**: Even though birds are creatures of habit, new items, new places, and new people will intrigue most birds. Keeping things fresh and new can spell F-U-N for bored birds.

## Your Bird's Defining Factors

You can determine in a general way what your bird may appreciate by considering these factors: species, age, and upbringing and present lifestyle. To determine what specifically will capture

This Jardine's parrot tries out a new perch. Branches and ropes add environmental enrichment to any cage or play area.

your bird's attention, take note of his reactions to various toys, games, and outings.

**Species**: Birds are not domesticated as dogs and cats are. Relatives of the bird that you have in your home still exist somewhere in the wild. Captive birds are only a few generations removed from their wild counterparts, so they still have all of the instincts of their ancestors. Do a little research on the habits of your species in the wild. Is your species of bird a ground feeder, or does it hang out in a rain forest canopy? What time of day is this species most active? What does it feed on in the wild? All of these aspects of your bird's species will give you some clues to what your bird may like to do, see, eat, and have. For example, a ground feeder such as the cockatiel may like playing with

Friendly fingers scratch a sweet white-bellied caique. Wild relatives of this parrot cutie still exist in the Amazon Basin in South America.

foraging toys at the bottom of the cage, while a canopy feeder such as an Amazon parrot may like his veggies strung on a birdy kabob at the top of the cage.

**Age**: Young birds may choose different items to play with than older birds will. They also tend to need a lot of activity and a large variety of environmental enrichment. Older birds, by contrast, may settle into a routine and not be as active as they were in their youth. They may prefer just a few specific items and so will not need as many toys as a younger bird will.

**Upbringing and lifestyle**: Is your bird a hand-fed sweetie pie? A parent-raised but hand-tamed friend? Skittish but social? Antisocial but talkative? A member of a bird couple or a flock? Part of your bird's temperament is based on how he was raised and the circumstances of his present life. A bird who's very attached to you (such as one you raised and hand-fed) will want a lot of social enrichment. A bird that had less hands-on play as he was growing up may need a lot more solo and environmental enrichment.

## ▼ Hand-Tamed Friend

A hand-raised bird is one who was taken from the nest when he or she was a baby and was hand-fed by a human. This type of bird is usually friendly if continually handled. A parent-raised bird is less likely to be immediately friendly and may require some extra taming.

# Illness or Hormones the Culprit?

When you are looking for the reason behind behavioral changes in a bird, the place to start is at an avian veterinarian's office. Many illnesses and even minor injuries can lead to changes in a bird's temperament, mood, and regular routine. In other instances, behavioral issues can be the result of a hormone surge in the spring, when daylight lasts longer than darkness. This time change can wreak havoc on a typically mild-mannered bird's personality. A mature male bird may become aggressive and bossy, and a female may become territorial and try to nest.

Expect excessive vocalization, unpredictability, and even biting this time of year. If you suspect hormones are an issue, cut your bird's daylight time to about nine or ten hours a day and see if that helps. When the clocks change again in the fall, your bird should return to normal. If he checks out as healthy and hormones aren't to blame, then it's time to improve his environment and add activities to enrich his life.

# Solo ENRICHMENT

Unless you have a "bird cam," you're not sure what your bird is doing when you're not home. Most likely he's sitting on a perch, picking food out of his dish, and chewing on some of his toys. Doesn't sound extremely entertaining, does it? Enrichment can turn the average perch potato into an acrobat, climbing and swinging about his enclosure; a scholar, figuring out knotty puzzles; and an archaeologist, digging for buried treasure. In this chapter, you will find some toys and activities to help keep your bird safely occupied and stimulated whenever he's flying solo.

## Foraging

*Foraging*, a hot birdy buzzword, forms the foundation for any good enrichment program. It is the best kind of solo activity because it mimics a bird's natural feeding behavior. Foraging experiments with parrots have shown that many prefer *contrafreeloading* behavior, meaning that they would rather seek out their food than eat from a dish of freely offered food. This gathering behavior is more natural for them and obviously more fulfilling. Try some foraging toys, or hide your bird's favorite treats in small packages or cups all around the cage. Once your bird gets the hang of it, you can hide some of his regular food as well.

**Foraging pods**: Some cages now come with foraging pod attachments to ensure that your bird is exposed to this important solo enrichment activity. To make your own foraging pods, fill little baskets or woven finch nests with goodies, and have your bird work to get the stuff out. Fruit and veggie "birdy kabobs" are also considered foraging opportunities because birds have to make an effort to get the food off the sticks. A birdy kabob is a hanging toy that you can thread with all kinds of healthy goodies. Place inedible desired objects (plastic rings and other baubles) along with food into foraging containers—this mixture will further motivate your bird to forage. If your birdcage doesn't have a foraging pod already, you can buy one (also called a foraging cage) at your local pet store or online.

**Foraging toys**: Any toy that makes a bird work for a reward is considered a foraging opportunity, which provides great mental and

# OK to Play with Food

Yes, birds should be encouraged to play with their food. Birds are natural foragers. They instinctively enjoy searching and rummaging through their treats and snacks. Give your bird lots of foods that he'll have fun tossing around. Try carrots cut into chips, large bunches of greens, grapes, lima beans, air-popped popcorn (no oil), garbanzo beans, and pitted cherries. Even if he doesn't eat everything, he will have fun playing with all the items.

physical stimulation. Try toys that are prefilled with treats or puzzle toys that make your bird move parts to retrieve a snack. (For specific toy ideas, see "Playing with Toys.")

**Wrapped dishes**: To make your bird's regular meals more fun, you can also simply wrap the food dish with a piece of tissue paper and poke holes in the top to allow your bird to see the food beneath. He will have to rip through the paper to eat the food. Once he gets used to the tissue paper, move up to construction paper to make the activity a little more challenging—and fun!

## Playing with Toys

Obviously, bird toys are on the top of the solo enrichment list. You can choose from a wide range of them at the pet store, make your own, or do both. For instance, birdy piñatas and toys that include paper and destructible woven materials are big fun for most birds. You'll have to replace these often, so you may want to learn to make them at home if you want to save money. Here are some pet store toys and homemade ones that may thrill your bored birdy.

## Toys from the Store

Pet stores are chock-full of toys that your bird may like to play with, from coils to swings, and they come in many bird-appealing materials, including rope and wood.

**Coils and "boings"**: Any coiled toy with the ability to bounce back, swing, or sway will entertain a bird. Coil toys made from rope or sisal tend to become bird favorites because they also can be used as perches.

**Foot toys**: Small foot toys should be a staple in every bird's toy box. Some birds like to roll on their backs and play footsie with small items, while others like to kick them around or

group them in a corner. Bird-approved whiffle balls, bell balls, acrylic toys, birdy dumbbells, and willow balls are all good choices.

**Grasses**: Woven grasses are safe and fun for a bird to pull apart, especially when a woven toy is filled with treats or other small toys. Many birds love crunchy and crinkly textures, so baskets and woven mats make perfect toys for birdy destruction.

**Knots**: Try toys with lots of rope, leather, and sisal knots, and watch your bird take on the challenge of unraveling them. Be sure to remove rope toys when they become frayed, and always trim long strands that may pose a tangling hazard.

**Noisy toys**: Birds love to make noise! Include toys with lots of safe bells and rattles. Please note that old-fashioned jingle bells

A swingin', singin' lovebird takes a ride on a beaded swing. Decorate swings with bells and rattles for ultimate birdy fun.

are dangerous for birds because they can get a beak or nail caught in a slot. Fortunately, most companies are making safer versions these days for birds, so just be sure that these are the ones you bring home. Clappers inside bells should be securely affixed and nontoxic. Other noisy toys include ones that play music and ones that record your voice and play it back with the push of a beak.

**Orbs**: Sphere-shaped toys made from rope or plastic that allow a bird to perch or crawl inside are often favorites.

**Puzzle toys**: Some intelligent birds thrive on figuring things out. Puzzle toys that hide food provide great stimulation.

**Swings**: Every parrot should have at least one swing, preferably one that includes toys and bells dangling from it.

**Wood toys**: Wood toys are great for birds—from a bird's perspective, everything looks better a little bit chewed. Choose wooden toys with bright, warm colors, and select soft, safe woods that are easy on the beak, such as cork, citrus, or cherry.

### Homemade Toys

Do you have a bird who's difficult to entertain? Do those expensive toys you spend your hard-earned money on sit in the cage untouched? Don't give up! Try some easy homemade toys—something as simple as a cheap toilet paper roll filled with nuts can entrance an otherwise uninterested bird. Some owners give up on birds who don't seem to want to play, but these birds probably haven't been provided with the kinds of toys that they like. Even if your bird likes store-bought toys, between visits to the pet store you can entertain—and enrich—your bird with several easy-to-make, homemade toys.

**Birdy kabob**: Find a safe birdy kabob holder at a bird or pet retailer (one that will not splinter or break into small pieces), and thread fruit and veggies on it for a fun daily snack/toy. You can also add inedible favorites that can be shredded—woven mats, willow balls, crumpled paper—to the kabob.

**Box o' fun**: Cut a cardboard box into various shapes, poke a hole in the center of each piece, string them on a piece of twine, and then tie your creation across the interior of the cage. Birds love to shred and chew this type of toy. Be careful that the twine you use doesn't become a noose—tie all knots very tightly.

**Chinese finger traps**: Remember those party favors called Chinese finger traps from your childhood? The cuff is a little woven tube that ensnares two fingers placed in opposite ends. Find a party store that sells these in bulk (get the woven natural-fiber type, not the plastic type), and string them on leather strands, weave them into the cage bars, or give them to your bird as foot toys that can be shredded. You can even fill them with nuts and other treats.

**Fruit basket**: Everyone likes to receive a fruit basket, don't they? Fill a little plastic or woven basket with some fresh fruits and veggies, arranged nicely as you would for a gift. Discard the uneaten portions before they spoil.

**Marble roll**: Place a mixture of jumbo marbles, nuts, popcorn, and a few foot toys into a shallow glass or Pyrex dish—a pie dish also

This lovebird can't get enough of his fruit birdy kabobs. Make mealtime a treat with foods you and your bird will love.

# Climbing

Cargo nets for birds to climb on have become very trendy, and they certainly won't be wasted on most birds, especially those species that spend the majority of their time in the canopy of the rain forest, such as macaws, lorikeets, and conures. Ladders, toys, and perches that hang from the top of the cage also give a swingin' bird some great exercise. When hanging ropes and cargo nets in your bird's cage, be sure that you cut off all loose strings and loops. If you don't get rid of these hazards, your bird may become entangled in the toy and be injured.

works nicely. Make sure that the dish you use isn't shallow enough for the marbles to easily roll out—that's the challenge!

**Paper wrap**: Roll treats inside white tissue paper, unbleached coffee filters, or white paper muffin/cupcake cups, then twist the ends so the packet looks like a piece of candy. Tie the ends with a small piece of sisal twine or other bird-safe material—you can even twist the tissue paper into thin strands, and use the paper itself as safe ties. Alternatively, wrap treats with craft paper or used (but clean) brown paper bags. Avoid rubber bands and plastic grocery ties, which can pose dangerous health hazards to your bird.

**Prank caller**: Drill a hole in a phone book, and hang the book on the side of the cage using sisal twine. The ink is safe, though your bird's feathers might get a little dirty from it. A bird who likes to shred will "go to town" shredding up the town! For a little bird, use a clean paperback book, preferably one you've already read!

**Variety toy box**: Use a small plastic food container as a daily toy box—fill it with plastic bottle caps, plastic straws, popcorn, empty plastic pen caps and barrels, Popsicle sticks, and plastic toys and beads. You can get a lot of great hard-plastic nursery toys at toy shops. To make the daily filling of the toy box easy, keep a cookie jar on your kitchen counter that's relegated to little baubles for your bird, and fill it up as you come across items that would be fun to play with. Just make sure that all the items are sized appropriately for your bird (*see page 33*).

## Toy Obsessions

There is some controversy or misunderstanding when it comes to toy obsession in birds. One school of thought says that the moment a bird becomes obsessed with a toy, the toy should be removed. Another school of thought says that it's cruel to remove a favored toy. As with most issues, there is a middle ground.

First, determine whether your bird is truly obsessed with the toy or just enjoying it. Obsession and hardy play are very different. A bird is obsessed with a toy when his behavior toward you or his cage mates changes as a result of an attachment to the toy. Perhaps the bird is protecting the toy aggressively or acting out a romance with it. Or maybe the bird is regurgitating for the toy (to feed it or romance it) so often that you fear for the bird's health. A bird who's just playing with a toy won't change his behavior toward you when the toy is "threatened" or constantly regurgitate for it.

This macaw may like his ball close by, but that doesn't mean he's toy obsessed. Big behavioral changes signal obsession.

**If your bird's toy buddy isn't a substitute mate and the bird's behavior hasn't changed— he just loves one particular toy over others— don't sweat it too much.**

If you suspect that your bird is becoming obsessed with a toy, try to determine the cause. Is the bird mature and is it springtime? Has the bird been prompted into breeding behaviors but has no mate? It's possible that no matter what you do, no matter how many toys you remove from your bird, he or she will still find something to "mate" with. This isn't a crisis; the behavior usually stops in the fall when natural daylight gets shorter. You can also use artificial lighting to prompt a bird out of breeding mode by allowing only nine to ten hours of light per day.

If your bird's toy buddy isn't a substitute mate and the bird's behavior hasn't changed—he just loves one particular toy over others—don't sweat it too much. It's like having a favorite pair of shoes or drinking from your favorite cup. Some birds also will sleep snuggled up with a favorite toy as a security blanket. This is not obsession, it's just habit, and having a habit isn't always negative.

# Toy Safety

Toys should always be appropriately sized for your bird. If the toy is too small, your bird could break it and injure himself. If the toy is too large, some of its parts could cause choking or pinch your bird's tiny feet and toes. Birds tend to like toys with pieces that are easily manipulated with the beak, so blocks and other elements should generally be smaller than the bird's head. Look for toys that are sturdy and washable. If you're not sure whether a certain item is appropriate for your particular bird, consult your veterinarian or a knowledgeable pet store employee.

# Social ENRICHMENT

There are few activities more fulfilling for a bird than one-on-one time with his favorite human—you! Playing with you, cuddling with you, and simply spending time in your presence will not only keep your bird active and occupied but also make him feel safe. Remember, most birds are naturally social creatures, and they don't do well in isolation. In this chapter, you'll find some fun, interactive activities that you and your bird can do together to enrich his life.

## Interactive Attention

Interactive play is when you handle your bird and interact directly with him. This includes having your bird ride around on your shoulder or hand, scratching him on the neck, talking to him and encouraging him to play with toys, and anything else you do together that entertains him (nail clipping does not count!). Your bird should get a minimum of an hour of direct play a day—even more if you can fit it into your schedule. The playtime does not have to be consecutive. Of course, only handle a bird who likes being handled! If your bird doesn't like interactive play, then spend time on indirect activities.

## Indirect Attention

Indirect attention is when you are in the room with your bird and he is contentedly playing with his toys by himself. The two of you are just hanging out. Put a cup filled with popcorn and a few bottle caps in the cage, or provide the bird with a new toy on his play gym. Now you can sit down to watch a couple of your favorite TV shows in

# **Shower** Time

If your bird likes water—or just hanging out with you—invest in a perch for your shower. The humidity of the shower will be good for your bird's skin and feathers, and your daily shower will be a great time to bond with your bird. You can compete for best shower-singing voice! Always supervise this activity, and make sure the water isn't too hot. Don't take a skittish bird, or an untamed one that can fly away from you, into the shower.

the same room. The bird can communicate with you with vocalizations or just take comfort from the knowledge that you're nearby. This way he can play contentedly and safely under your watchful eye, especially when you're not sure about the safety of a new toy or when he's outside the cage. Give your bird several hours of indirect attention daily.

## Hands-on Training

Doing some simple training exercises with your bird gives him some dedicated hands-on time and strengthens your bond with each other. Training can be as simple as teaching or reinforcing the cue *step up* (teaching your bird to step onto your finger or hand) and as complex as teaching your bird to dunk a tiny basketball or solve puzzles. Try at least two ten-minute training sessions daily. Be sure to make

This content cockatiel enjoys some hands-on attention. It's important to spend at least an hour a day interacting with your bird.

them fun! For more training material, see the resources at the end of the book.

## Mealtimes

Sharing mealtimes is very enriching for your bird, an animal that would rarely eat alone in the wild. Try placing your bird on a tabletop perch or a T-stand and sharing your food with him. Alternatively, fill a dish with his food and just eat at the same time—he in his cage and you nearby. As simple as it may seem, dining together is one of the best social activities you can do with your bird.

## Bird Company

Whether or not your particular bird will accept a bird companion is a judgment call only you can make. To discover whether your bird

These conures make great buddies, but not all birds will be this friendly. Find out if your species of bird plays well with others.

is more of a people's bird or a bird's bird, try a birdy playdate. This must be done with great care, however. Before introducing two birds, read up on whether your species of bird is likely to respond well to a companion of the same species or to one of another species. For example, many South American species, such as conures and Amazons, take well to meeting other South American species, but many midsize to large African species, such as African greys, may not appreciate being presented with a new birdy companion, no matter what his ancestors' origins.

If your research indicates that your bird may be receptive to a particular companion, then begin the introduction by placing the birds' cages or play stands near each other. (Be especially careful when introducing a larger bird to a smaller one because a large bird can seriously injure or kill a small bird.) If there's immediate aggression, such as lunging, hissing, or biting, stop the playdate right away, and don't bother trying again with that particular would-be companion. If the birds touch beaks, vocalize to each other, and preen each other, you've made a good match. Always make sure that birds exposed to other birds have recently been given a clean bill of health from an avian veterinarian. And always supervise two birds when they are together—even when they appear to get along.

As noted above, many birds appreciate a companion of the same species, and some birds will even bond with birds of other species—just make sure they don't have an opportunity to start nesting.

A pair of conures get to know each other a little better. Always supervise birdy playdates even if your birds seem to be getting along.

# Environmental ENRICHMENT

Enriching your bird's environment is about providing him with sights, sounds, and items that will stimulate some of his natural instincts. The first part of enriching your bird's environment is to improve his housing. That can mean a better view of the world, more sound in the air, a special place to play, plenty of light, and larger housing. Permanently move your bird's cage into a room that attracts a lot of family members; however, keep the cage out of high-traffic spots (that is, the pathways people usually take in and out of the room).

## A Room with a View

A boring view is pure monotony for a bird. Try to give your bird something interesting to watch. Most birds enjoy a window view, at least part of the time. If the cage isn't close enough to a window for your bird to see what's going on outside, move the cage closer for part of the day, or have an additional window-view cage. A nervous bird may not want to see all of the activity outside, but a secure bird may be quite entertained by the neighbors. Offer your bird an area to retreat to—such as a covered part of the cage—in case something outside frightens him. Remember not to place your bird's cage next to a window full time because of temperature fluctuations and sleep disturbances.

A tank filled with colorful fish (or fake fish and lots of bubbles) can be a fun distraction as well. Just make sure that the tank is out of the bird's reach and is completely covered; it can pose a drowning risk when you let your bird out for playtime or if your bird gets out of his cage unsupervised.

## A Symphony of Sound

Background noise mimics a bird's wild environment. The rain forest, savanna, or scrubland is never quiet except when a predator is present. Then all of the prey animals instantly shut up and listen for the predator's next move—they don't want to risk being noticed and becoming a midnight snack. Quiet equals danger.

Reassure your bird by being his personal disc jockey or radio and TV programmer. Choose shows that you think your bird will like, perhaps talk shows with lots of chattering or

These cockatiels get a great view from their secondary cage in the living room. Place your bird's cage in a room that attracts family members.

# Taming Wanderlust

Unfortunately, if your bird is a wanderer, it's very difficult to quell the behavior. Picking the bird up will positively reinforce the behavior because he gains personal interaction with you—but you have to pick him up if he's wandering! For a more impersonal approach, you can try to pick him up by having him step up onto a stick or perch, making no eye contact and not speaking to him, and return him to his cage. Come back a few minutes later, and try again to place him in a play area. This takes a lot of patience and may not work for every wanderer. If your bird continues to wander, make sure to supervise him carefully.

# Your bird should have a play area away from his cage, especially if he's a tame family bird.

stations playing classical or other music. (I once knew a cockatiel who was nuts for reggae.)

Keeping a tabletop fountain nearby provides relaxing background noise for a bird. Running water simulates a type of sound he would hear in the wild. For the trendy bird, a fountain also adds a bit of Zen spa atmosphere. Use only a shallow tabletop fountain, and don't allow your bird to drink from it.

## A Time for Play

Your bird should have a play area away from his cage, especially if he's a tame family bird. Some cages come equipped with a play top; if yours doesn't, you can purchase a play gym and place it in an area where you can observe your bird while he's out of the cage. Or you can have both the play top and play gym! Most of the medium- to large-size birds love their play areas and won't wander. However, there are always those who feel that it's a lot more fun climbing the curtains or hopping down to the floor to follow you around the house. If this is the case, you can try to make the play area more fun to keep your bird there. Include more toys, and feed your bird his favorite treats only in the play area. If your bird still insists on wandering, try the suggestions in "Taming Wanderlust" (*opposite page*).

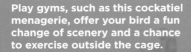

Play gyms, such as this cockatiel menagerie, offer your bird a fun change of scenery and a chance to exercise outside the cage.

Play stands (or parrot gyms) for birds are not cheep . . . er, cheap, so if you want to save a few bucks, make one yourself. Start with a clean 5-gallon plastic bucket for a large parrot and a smaller bucket for a little bird. Fill the bucket with plaster of paris, then stick some tree branches into it—choose safe, nontoxic branches that have both horizontal and vertical areas for your bird to perch on and climb. Plaster of paris is made from calcium carbonate, the same material used in mineral blocks, and it is safe for birds unless it has any additives. (Be sure to check the ingredients on the packaging, or if they are not listed, contact the manufacturer.) Tape the branches to the bucket until the plaster sets. When the branches are

firmly in place, hang toys on them. Finally, cover the bucket with silk vines or clean moss to hide it from view. When the branches get worn out or chewed, you can make a new bucket stand for less than ten dollars.

## Lights for Life

Natural lighting is essential for avian health. It stimulates natural processes in a bird's body. Most birds have a preen gland at the base of the tail feathers that produces an oil birds spread through their feathers while preening. This oil turns into vitamin D, an important nutrient, when ultraviolet light hits it, and the bird ingests the oil once again while preening. If your bird doesn't receive direct sunlight (or receives it only through a window, which blocks most ultraviolet rays), purchase special UV-lighting bulbs and lamps so your bird gets this important health benefit. These lights also help your bird's vision and promote good feather health. A bird receiving no natural light and no supplemental bird lighting can become deficient in vitamin D.

Additionally, you can take your bird outside in a safe cage or carrier. Some birds take well to this and some don't. If your bird is a little fearful of being put inside a carrier, help him

# Perches and Branches

Does your bird have interesting perches? Perches are to birds like shoes are to many women—we need a lot of them, and they have to be nice! Try a variety of perches and even natural branches if you can find unsprayed trees in your area. Check with a veterinarian to make sure a specific type of tree is safe for birds. Branches from apple, cherry, and citrus trees are safe, as are those from ash, aspen, palm, and pecan trees. But juniper, mango, oleander, and walnut branches are not. Size is not an issue—just make sure the branches don't take over the entire cage!

Even birds with trimmed wing feathers, such as this budgie, appreciate a chance to stretch their wings.

## Allowing a bird some time outdoors in a safe enclosure during nice weather is a real gift for a companion bird.

adjust to it by putting him inside with a treat for a few minutes a day, making the experience as positive as possible. Eventually he'll get used to it, and you can take him outside for a sunbath. Just make sure the carrier or cage is securely closed and that he has fresh water in case he gets too warm. Never leave a bird alone in direct sunlight where he can't find a shady spot.

### A Place to Soar

An aviary gives your bird an opportunity to fly, which, of course, is what birds are meant to do! Even if you can't keep your bird in a large enclosure all of the time, build something as large as possible in a well-protected area to allow your bird some flying time—or at least give him the temporary feeling of not having bars directly over his head. Allowing a bird some time outdoors in a safe enclosure during nice weather is a real gift for a companion bird.

### ⬇ Outside Activities

Playing outside is not safe for birds unless they are in a bird-safe carrier or cage and are under close supervision. Just make sure they don't get overheated or fearful.

# Variance
# ENRICHMENT

**N**ot all birds love adventures, but some of them will delight in vacations away from the cage, even if the destination is only as far as the porch or backyard. As noted in the last chapter, seeing new things, hearing new sounds, and feeling the sunshine on his feathers all are highly enriching for a secure bird. Here are a few ideas for enriching your bird's life through changes in scenery and environment away from the house as well as around it.

## Field Trips

Most secure, human-attached birds love a field trip, even if they're not going that far. Some of them love adventures to the mall, to outdoor cafés, to parks, and to other safe outdoor locations. Some birds even love riding in the car and looking out the window at the passing scenery just as the family dog does! Confirm that pets, specifically birds, are allowed wherever you take your bird by calling ahead. Be sure that the place is safe from potential hazards, such as your bird flying away or being attacked by another animal. In most cases, the safest way to take your bird outside is in a bird-safe carrier. Even birds with recent wing-feather trims can become spooked and fly in a panic.

# Field Trip Safety

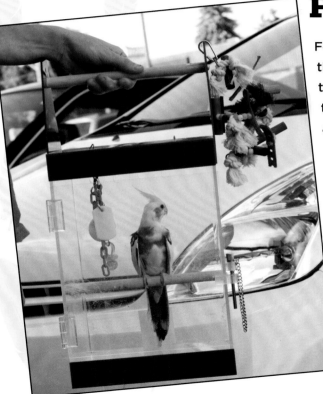

For birds, safety always trumps fun. If the flight feathers on his wings are not trimmed, be extremely cautious when taking your bird outside of the house; always use a safe and secure carrier. A carrier is a good idea for a bird with trimmed wing feathers as well, at least until you get inside your safe destination. A safe bird carrier is made from hard plastic or metal. Don't use a soft carrier for your bird or he may chew his way out! A dog or cat carrier will do, but a bird-specific carrier usually has an opening at the top and has places to put food and water dishes.

A cockatiel relaxes with his favorite human. Add variance to your bird's life by including him in everything you do.

# Simply hanging out with your bird on a nice day outside—as a routine— is great enrichment.

## Variation at Home

If you don't feel comfortable taking your bird on a field trip, you can still provide some variation at home.

**Porch perch potato**: Ah, lazy days on an enclosed porch with a glass of lemonade and a bird by your side. What better way to enhance your bird/person bond and enrich your bird's life. Simply hanging out with your bird on a nice day outside—as a routine—is great enrichment.

**Room rotation**: If you really want to give your bird a thrill, put a play gym or tabletop gym in every room of your house and include him in everything you do. All you have to do is move him from room to room and give him indirect attention by hanging out together. BFFFs! Best feathered friends forever!

**Toy rotation**: Some birds like variety in their toys, and they will treat a toy as a novelty if you take it away for an extended period of time and then return it. For these birds, keep two or three sets of homemade toys and store-bought toys on hand and rotate them monthly.

# Enriched Bird, HAPPY BIRD

Once you find your bird's favorite enrichment activities, whether they be solo, social, environmental, or variance, try to stick with them and make them a regular part of his day. Remember to be consistent—your bird will notice when you skip a regular activity, and he'll find a way to tell you (maybe a very loud way). You'll have a much happier bird on your hands if you go the extra birdy mile to give him as many enrichment opportunities as possible. He will thank you with fewer behavior issues, fewer veterinary bills, and lots of fun and love.

# About the Author

Nikki Moustaki, freelance writer and animal trainer, has published more than forty books, primarily on the care and training of pets, and has been a bird fancier for two decades. Nikki hosts two pet-related shows in Miami Beach, Florida, and hosted the NBC/MSN online show *The Celebrity Pet Dish*. Her Web site, The Pet Postcard Project (www.petpostcardproject .com), raises awareness, food, and funds for shelter animals. Nikki splits her time between New York City and Miami Beach with her three dogs and three parrots. You can reach Nikki at www.nikkimoustaki.com.

## Resources

### General Organizations

The Association of Avian Veterinarians: www.aav.org

National Cage Bird Show Club: www.ncbs.org

### Magazines and Books

*BIRD TALK* magazine: www.birdchannel.com

*Ask the Bird Keeper*, by Marc Morrone, BowTie Press

*Budgies*, by Angela Davids, BowTie Press

*Cockatiels*, by Angela Davids, BowTie Press

*Conures*, by Nikki Moustaki, BowTie Press

*Lovebirds*, by Nikki Moustaki, BowTie Press

*Why Do Cockatiels Do That?* by Nikki Moustaki, BowTie Press

*Why Do Parakeets Do That?* by Nikki Moustaki, BowTie Press